KU-495-917

OLYMPIC LIBRARY

Ancient Olympics

Richard Tames

WANDSWORTH PUBLIC LIBRARIES
09
05/96

Heinemann

C
796
.48
TAME

500038974

First published in Great Britain by Heinemann Publishers
(Oxford) Ltd
Halley Court, Jordan Hill, Oxford OX2 8EJ

MADRID ATHENS PARIS
FLORENCE PRAGUE WARSAW
PORTSMOUTH NH CHICAGO SAO PAULO
SINGAPORE TOKYO MELBOURNE AUCKLAND
IBADAN GABORONE JOHANNESBURG

© Richard Tames 1996

All rights reserved. No part of this publication may be reproduced, stored in a retrieval system, or transmitted in any form
or by any means, electronic, mechanical, photocopying, recording, or otherwise without either the prior written
permission of the Publishers or a licence permitting restricted copying in the United Kingdom issued by the Copyright
Licensing Agency Ltd, 90 Tottenham Court Road, London W1P 9HE

Designed by VAP Group Ltd
Illustrations by Oxford Illustrators (p20, p23).
Printed in the UK by Jarrold Printing, Norwich

00 99 98 97 96
10 9 8 7 6 5 4 3 2 1

ISBN 0 431 05943 8

British Library Cataloguing in Publication Data

Tames, Richard
  Ancient Olympics. — (Olympic Library)
  I. Title II. Series
  796.480938

Acknowledgements
The Publishers would like to thank the following for permission to reproduce photographs:
Robert Harding Picture Library: p.4; British Museum: p.5; Bildarchiv preussischer kulturbesitz: p.6; The Metropolitan
Museum of Art, Rogers Fund, 1908: p.8; Ancient Art & Architecture Collection: p.9; H.L. Pierce Fund, Courtesy, Museum
of Fine Arts, Boston: p.10; Wirmer Fotoarchiv: p.11; AKG/Erich Lessing: p.13; Deutsches Archäologisches Institut-Athen:
p.13; Ancient Art & Architecture Collection: p.14; Ancient Art & Architecture Collection: p.15; Wirmer Fotoarchiv: p.16;
AKG Berlin/Erich Lessing: p.17; Deutsches Archäologisches Institut-Athen: p.18; The Metropolitan Museum of Art,
Rogers Fund, 1949: p.19; Robert Harding Picture Library: p.20; Ancient Art & Architecture Collection: p.23; Deutsches
Archäologisches Institut-Athen: p.24; Ancient Art & Architecture Collection: p.25; Hulton Deutsch: p.26, 27; Colorsport:
p.28; Richard Tames: p.29.

Cover photographs reproduced with permission of the British Museum and Professional Sports.
Cover designed by Brigitte Willgoss.

Our thanks to Mr Robert Paul of the US Olympic Committee and Dr Stephen Ridd for their comments in the preparation
of this book.

Olympic rings logo reproduced with the permission of the International Olympic Committee.

Every effort has been made to contact copyright holders of any material reproduced in this book.
Any omissions will be rectified in subsequent printings if notice is given to the Publisher.

Contents

The Will to Win

A natural stadium? Olympia today, showing fallen pillars of the temple of Zeus.

The Aim of the Games

Games are meant to be fun, but the ancient Olympics were deadly serious. All that mattered was winning. There were no second or third prizes. Players either won or lost. Winners were heroes who became famous – and rich, even though no prize money was given.

Some used their fame to help them become politicians. The others usually became trainers.

Greeks thought that their gods enjoyed watching the sports, and this gave a sense of glory to the winner. The Games were held in honour of Zeus, the king of the gods. He had a special temple at Olympia.

Deadly Serious

The Games really were deadly. Chariot races involving up to forty chariots, on a two-way course without a barrier, led to head-on collisions and huge pile-ups. Horse races were run on the ground churned up by the chariots, on horses without shoes, ridden by jockeys without saddles or stirrups, so there were many falls, with the risk of being trampled to death. Boxing matches sometimes went on for so long that the judges would settle a fight by making the boxers hit each other in turn until one or the other collapsed or gave in.

The fiercest event was the **pankration**, a combination of boxing and wrestling in which almost anything except eye-gouging and biting was allowed. One favoured tactic was to break all the opponent's fingers and then finish him off when he was helpless to fight back.

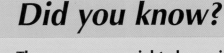

Did you know?

There were no weight classes in the combat sports, so almost inevitably they were won by the biggest men. If one man killed another, the dead man was declared the winner.

Fair Play?

Greek ideas of fair play may seem rather strange. In chariot and horse races the owner, not the rider, was declared the winner, which meant that a horse which crossed the finish line first, but without its rider, could still win. In ancient times there were no events for women – and they weren't even allowed to watch, as they had no standing in the community. They were supposed to look after their homes and families.

The Greatest Achievement

The ancient Greeks are famous for their great achievements in art, science, mathematics, medicine and drama. But if anyone had asked a Greek what they thought was the greatest thing the Greeks had ever done, they would probably have said the Olympic Games.

The illustration on the vase shows boxers with leather-bound fists fighting toe to toe.

Gods and Legends – How the Games Began

Legend and Literature

Greek legend tells how Heracles was set twelve tasks as a punishment. One was to clean out the huge, filthy stables of King Augeas. Augeas promised him a reward if he succeeded. Heracles cleaned the stables by digging a trench to make a river flow through them. When Augeas tried to cheat him out of his reward, Heracles killed the king and founded the Olympic Games to celebrate his victory. This is only one of many stories about how the Games started.

The first and longest account of games in Greek literature is in Homer's poem, the *Iliad*. It was written in the ninth century BC but is set at the time of the Trojan War. In this poem, when the Greek hero Achilles' friend Patroclus is killed, he organizes games to mark his funeral.

Wrestlers grapple while a goddess looks on – carrying a trainer's switch! Notice the towel and jar of water for afterwards.

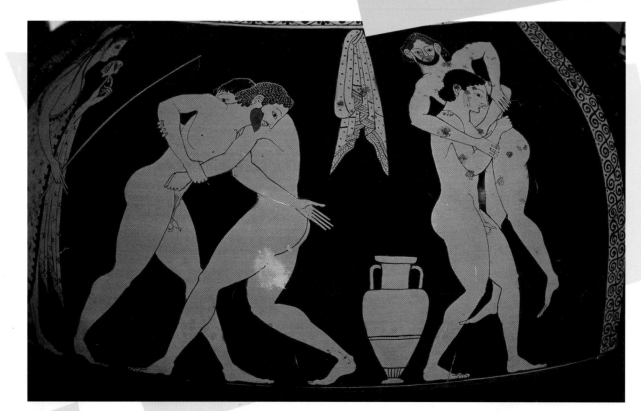

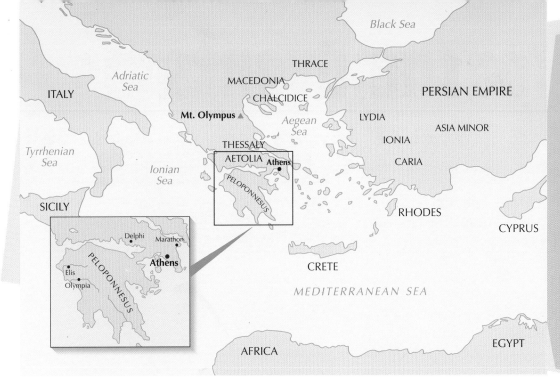

Eventually far more Greeks lived overseas, especially in Asia Minor (Turkey), southern Italy and Sicily than in Greece itself. But Olympia's location near the coast made access easier than if the Games had been held in the centre of the country.

Archaeology

Results of **excavations** by **archaeologists** suggest that games might have been held at Olympia as early as 1370BC. However, traditionally the first Olympic Games took place in 776BC. Olympia is on the western side of Peloponnese, the southern part of the Greek mainland. The Greeks thought of it as a holy place.

The Gods of Olympus

The Greeks believed that their gods were in many ways like humans, with loves and quarrels. They were also thought to interfere in human affairs. To keep the gods on their side they thought it was advisable to show them respect through prayer and **sacrifices**. This could be especially important to athletes.

When lots of competitors wanted to enter an event it was necessary to organize **heats** to choose finalists. The names of those taking part in each heat were drawn by **lot**.

Many athletes would pray or sacrifice an animal in the hope of being drawn against weaker opponents.

The Olympic Games did have a definite religious side to them. During the Games, wars between different Greek states were set aside so that athletes from all over the Greek world could attend. Solemn sacrifices were an important part of the proceedings. Competitors swore a sacred **oath** not to cheat.

Cheats who were found out had to pay for building a statue of Zeus, king of the gods. In the thousand year history of the ancient Olympics

Did you know?

The Olympics were so important to the ancient Greeks that they based their calendar on them. The four year period between Games was known as an Olympiad.

7

The Events

The first, and for a long time, the only event was a sprint. The distance was one **stadion** (from which we get the word 'stadium') which was 185 m (202 yards). In 724BC a second race of two stadia was added and in 720BC a much longer one of 24 stadia (4.4 km or 2.76 miles) was introduced.

Over the course of their history the Games involved 23 different events, though these were never all held on the same occasion. As new ones were added some old ones were dropped. Because the Olympics were held in honour of Zeus, king of the gods, who lived above the Earth on Mount Olympus, there were no swimming events. Swimming contests were part of other games, particularly the Isthmian Games. Events in the Olympics included:

❖ Contests for **heralds** and trumpeters
Heralds travelled throughout the Greek-speaking world, announcing the three-month **truce** which made it safe to travel to the Games. They also took a leading part in the actual events by announcing winners and helping to organize ceremonial processions of athletes, judges and representatives of all the cities taking part.

A long-jumper landing. Athletes would land in the skamma, a bed of earth broken up and raked smooth for the athlete to land without damage and leave a clear imprint.

❖ Chariot racing with mules
Drivers of horse-chariots stood up and were only protected by a knee-high barrier on the front and sides of their chariot. Mule-drivers sat down and couldn't go as fast. As this was less exciting for spectators, mule-racing events were dropped after a while.

❖ Running in full armour
This event reminded spectators that Games began as a training for war, but over the centuries it became rather a joke, although it was never dropped. It was less graceful than the other running races and because swords and javelins were not carried, to avoid accidents, it was far less dangerous than the combat sports.

Running in armour. The competitors are shown wearing heavy, bronze leg-guards which were later discarded for this event.

The Greeks invented the multiple contest known as **pentathlon** – running, jumping, **discus**, javelin and wrestling. Nowadays this is thought to be the supreme test of an athlete, but for the Greeks it was the least prized event. Chariot and horse races ranked top because only rulers and rich **aristocrats** could afford to put in entries. (They didn't usually take part themselves.) As more events were added to the Games **professional** athletes, who could afford long periods of training, came to specialize in just one event. So the pentathlon was often left to the **amateurs**.

Did you know?

'Jumping' meant the long jump, never the high jump. This seemed natural to Greeks as their mountainous countryside had many streams and ditches which a traveller might need to leap across, but there were no fences or hedges.

Judges, Rules and Prizes

A long-jumper using weights curves his body forward at the moment of take-off. His trainer has a switch lifted, to punish him for a bad landing. Another athlete uses a weight as a dumb-bell for exercise.

Judges

Judges wore purple robes so that everyone could see who they were. They were under oath to be fair and were not allowed to be contestants themselves. Judges were always chosen from the people of Elis, a town near Olympia. As Elis was only a small place, whose main business was the Games, its people were trusted to be neutral. Because Greek cities were fierce rivals it would have been more difficult for everyone to have faith in a judge from a large, powerful city like Athens or Corinth.

Judging really did involve judgement. There was no time-keeping system. After each event judges would confer and then vote in secret to decide the winner. They were under oath to keep their conferences secret.

Rules

Contestants had to be free sons of free-born Greeks. Slaves were not allowed to take part. Athletes competed naked but were allowed to rub themselves with oil and fine sand.

The use of some sorts of equipment was allowed. Long-jumpers carried hand-held weights which they swung forward, to give them more **momentum**, and then swung back to help them make a clean landing. Boxers wound strips of leather round their hands and forearms, but left their fingers free. Javelin-throwers used a finger-**thong** which gave added length to their throw and made the javelin spin, keeping its flight straight.

Athletes who broke the rules could be fined heavily or even whipped. This shows how seriously the Games were taken, because normally in the Greek world only slaves could be punished by whipping.

Did you know?

Because Olympic winners were heroes in their home cities they were often rewarded generously by being let off taxes, given pensions or being allowed to eat free at the town hall. The greatest had statues put up in their honour.

Prizes

Winners were rewarded only with a wreath of olive leaves cut from a sacred tree, which grew near the temple of Zeus at Olympia. It was the honour of winning that mattered.

A javelin-thrower using a thong under the watchful eye of his trainer.

The Great Gathering

The games held at Olympia began as a simple running race held on a single day. By 632BC they lasted for five days. This was how the programme was organized.

Day One

In the morning, competitors and judges gathered before the statue of Zeus and swore not to cheat. This ceremony was followed by the first contests – running, wrestling and boxing for boys. There was also time for spectators to visit temples to make private prayers and sacrifices. In the afternoon poets, historians and politicians made speeches or read aloud from their writings. Many spectators went sightseeing or had reunions with old friends. Others watched the jugglers, dancers and conjurors who came to amuse the huge crowds.

Day Two

The morning began with a procession of competitors, followed by chariot-races and horse-races at the track known as the **hippodrome**. A barrier protected the crowd from bolting horses or chariots which ran out of control. The afternoon was taken up with the pentathlon. The day's events were rounded off with a parade of winners, singing of victory songs and feasting.

Day Three

The morning was entirely taken up by a huge procession of judges, competitors and **ambassadors**, followed by the sacrifice of a hundred oxen. In the afternoon there were foot-races and in the evening a public banquet.

Day Four

This day was devoted to the combat sports – wrestling, boxing, **pankration** and running in full armour.

Day Five

The closing ceremonies involved a procession of the winners to the Temple of Zeus, where they were crowned with olive wreaths and showered with flowers.

This was followed by a last feast with music and dancing.

The illustration on the vase shows Athena decorating a victorious athlete with bands.

There were many fine temples and offices for officials at Olympia but few facilities for athletes or spectators. The main gymnasium is tucked away in the top corner at the far right.

Did you know?

All Greeks, whether they lived in Greece itself or in one of the Greek colonies scattered from the Black Sea to Sicily, knew Olympia. It was like a combination of national sports centre and sacred cathedral – the place everyone wanted to visit at festival time.

Circuits and Champions

The Olympic Games were the most famous games of all and a victory at Olympia was more prized than any other. But their success inspired so many other places to hold their own games that professional athletes could travel non-stop from one to another in the hope of picking up prizes. By 500BC there were about fifty games, by AD100 there were over 300. There were two types of games – sacred and prize.

The professional athletes were almost always specialists in one or at most two events. In a thousand years only half a dozen athletes ever won three different events in the Olympics.

Sacred Games

By 550BC three other sacred games had been founded which, with the Olympics, made up 'the Circuit'.

❖ The Pythian Games
These were held at Delphi to honour Apollo, and included musical contests as well as athletics. Winners got a laurel wreath. The Pythian Games were held the year before the Olympic Games and survived until the fourth century AD.

A woman athlete. In non-Olympic years foot-races for women were staged in honour of Hera, wife of Zeus. Competitors ran in three age-groups over five-sixths of the distance run by men.

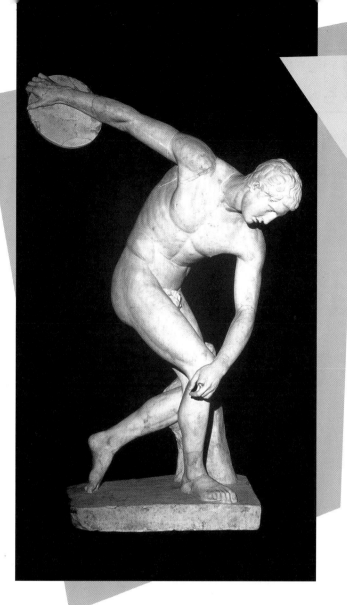

Stooping to throw the discus. The style of this statue was widely copied by both Greeks and Romans. It represents the ideal of absolute physical perfection.

Prize Games

When the heroes in Homer's *Iliad* competed in games, the winners were rewarded with prizes of horses, slaves and bronze **cauldrons**. At prize games, victors usually, but not always, got money, ranging from 600 to 6000 **drachmas** – which equalled from two to twenty years' wages for an ordinary soldier. Some athletes won enough to have a comfortable retirement or even to go into politics.

❖ The Isthmian Games
These were held at the port of Corinth in honour of the sea-god Poseidon. They included both athletics and music and were held in the same year as the Olympic Games and again in the second year after them. The prize was a crown of dried wild celery. They also ended in the fourth century AD.

❖ The Nemean Games
These were held at Nemea, south-west of Corinth, to honour Zeus, and were staged in the same year as the Isthmian Games. Winners also received a crown of wild celery.

Did you know?

The Panathenaea was an annual festival to honour Athena, guardian goddess of Athens. Eventually it was celebrated every fourth year as a rival to the Olympics. Winners were awarded jars of olive oil, decorated with pictures of their event and of the goddess Athena.

Sporting Legends

Sporting heroes were famed throughout the Greek world. Statues of them were put up in public places, showing them as examples of the physical perfection and noble character that anyone would wish to be like.

Often sporting heroes were followed in victory by members of their own family. A soldier, Demaratus, won the first ever race in full armour and then won the second. His son won the pentathlon twice, and *his* son won the wrestling twice.

Did you know?

The Greeks used to love stories about Olympic heroes, like Milo of Croton, who won the wrestling seven times. On one occasion he picked up a full-grown bull, carried it around the stadium at Olympia – to the astonishment of the crowd – then had it killed and ate it all the same day.

This bronze statue of a boxer shows the real price of sporting fame – scars and a cauliflower ear.

A Hero's Revenge

Theagenes of Thasos was probably the most famous Greek athlete of his time. In 468BC he won the boxing, wrestling and **pankration**. In the course of his career he was said to have won over 1400 victories in different games. He claimed to be a descendant of Heracles himself and it was said that when he was only nine he had carried off a bronze statue of his ancestor from the market place in Thasos. Theagenes' success meant that a statue was put up in his honour.

After Theagenes died one of his old opponents was still so enraged by his defeat that he came each night to thrash the statue – until it toppled over and killed him. When the dead man's children cried out for revenge the statue was tried in court and condemned to be thrown into the sea.

From then on nothing went right in Thasos. A terrible heat-wave killed the crops in the fields. In despair the Thasians asked the **Oracle** at Delphi what they should do. The priestess, who acted as a mouthpiece for the god, Apollo, advised them to bring back to Thasos anyone who had been sent away. It took the Thasians years to track them all down but nothing got better. Then the Oracle reminded them they had forgotten Theagenes. When his statue was caught in a fisherman's net the Thasians eagerly hauled it up and put it back in the market-place – and their fields grew fine crops once more.

There was probably some truth and a lot of fiction in this story. It shows how much the Greeks believed there was no clear line between the worlds of the gods and humans.

Wrestlers practise as their trainers watch and encourage them.

Trainers and Training

The Gymnasium

Every Greek city had at least one gymnasium, paid for out of taxes. Rich citizens and ambitious politicians often gave money to support a gymnasium. They also paid athletics **scholarships** to promising athletes from families too poor to support them during months of training.

The biggest gymnasium in the Greek world was at Pergamum in Asia Minor – which also had five other gymnasia!

The gymnasium was a place where young men could train for sports and practise with weapons. It was a place where they could meet their friends and hear their teachers giving lectures. Facilities would include exercise-rooms with punching-bags, outdoor grounds for races, baths for cleaning up afterwards, perhaps a library and a garden where they could relax, and an altar for sacrifices to the gods.

The Trainers

No-one pretended that training was anything but hard work. Surviving examples of trainers' handwriting suggests most were tough former athletes who had come up the hard way. Their pay would only have been the same as an average craftsman.

Trainers were expected to have the skill to coach. They also needed expert knowledge of massage, **hygiene** and how to treat sports injuries. Most regular doctors thought that trainers were ignorant men who often did more harm than good. Trainers thought doctors were full of useless book-learning, with no real experience of how the human body actually worked. Doctors rarely had anything to do with either gymnasia or the Games.

Did you know?

Diet was thought to be important, as well as exercise. Most Greeks ate a light diet of bread, cheese, fruit and vegetables. But athletes in the combat sports learned to build up their bodies by eating huge amounts of meat.

Training

Athletes wanting to go in for the Olympics had to commit themselves to a ten-month course of preparation to reach the entry standard. They had to arrive at Olympia at least a month beforehand. This gave them time to recover from their journey, which might have taken weeks by land and sea. But recovery did not mean relaxing, because they had to go through a further bout of intensive training under the eyes of the Olympic judges themselves. Trainers were allowed to accompany athletes to their events and shout advice and encouragement from the sidelines.

Boxers limbering up to flute music. Greek athletes were supposed to be graceful as well as tough.

Spectators

Getting There

Throughout their history, admission to the Games was free. However, the expense and dangers of travel in the ancient world meant that the only poor people likely to attend came from the Peloponnese. Rulers and ambassadors, by contrast, travelled in style with hundreds of attendants. One reason for going was so that the powerful people in each Greek city could show off to each other. The Games also provided a convenient occasion for secret discussions between different cities so that they could plot against their rivals.

Staying There

There was no town as such at Olympia. The nearest town, Elis, was almost 60 km (35 miles) away, so there was no possibility of staying there and travelling to Olympia each day. There was a luxury hotel for visiting officials and VIPs, but nothing for the ordinary traveller. So most people simply slept out in the open. The better-off had tents or temporary wooden huts put up for them.

Wonder of the World. The mighty statue of Zeus was removed to Constantinople in the fifth century AD where it was destroyed in a fire in 426.

Remains of the seating can still be seen at the site of the stadium at Olympia.

Food was bought from stall-holders and **pedlars**. Because the River Alpheus didn't dry up in summer and there were some springs, there was enough water to drink. While competitors could bathe, bathing was a problem for visitors, and so was **sanitation**. The discomforts of Olympia were so well known that everyone knew the story of a grumbling slave whose master threatened to take him to the Games if he didn't stop.

Seeing the Games

The stadium at Olympia could take about 40 000 spectators. Seating was provided only for judges. Ordinary spectators had to stand or sit on the surrounding hills. Although the Games took place in very hot July weather it was forbidden to wear a hat in case it blocked someone's view.

Did you know?

Apart from the sports, banquets and entertainers, there were also buildings and statues to see. The most famous was the temple housing the massive (12 m) gold and ivory statue of Zeus made by the sculptor Phidias. Greeks ranked it as one of the Seven Wonders of the World. Beside it there was a much smaller (2 m) figure of Nike, the Goddess of Victory.

The End of the Olympics

Decline ...

Greece became part of the Roman empire in 146BC but the Olympic Games went on without interruption. Roman peace and Roman respect for Greek culture meant that even more people wanted to come to the Olympics and felt safe to travel there.

The mad Roman emperor Nero decided to enter the Olympics but was too busy to get to the 211th Games, in AD65, so he ordered them to be postponed. He then ordered contests for **tragedians** and singers, which only he entered, and therefore won. He also won the chariot race, even though he fell off his chariot and failed to finish. A year later he was murdered and the whole 211th Games were declared invalid.

This illustration from a Greek vase shows athletes practising.

The Roman writer Pausanias visited Olympia around AD170, when the stadium had been renovated for the last time. He then wrote the first guide-book in the world.

It contained many stories from the history of the Olympics, listed some two hundred statues to be seen there and warned visitors to beware of the local guides.

... And Fall

The Olympics certainly continued until AD261, but after that it is less certain that they were held regularly or that they remained free of **corruption**. The Romans were less interested in real athletic contests, and focused on bloody combats. The Greek games were organized basically for the benefit of the gods. Roman games at first were for the gods, but changed to be for the benefit of the spectators. It was the difference between sport and show business.

The rise of Christianity finished off the ancient Olympics. Christian leaders disapproved of the athletes' nakedness and the Greeks' interest in the perfection of the body, rather than the soul. The Games were also hated because their sacrifices honoured pagan gods. In AD393 the Olympics were finally abolished by the Christian Emperor Theodosius the Great.

Did you know?

In AD 426 the Temple of Zeus at Olympia was burned down, possibly on the orders of Theodosius II. In the fifth and sixth centuries the actual site of Olympia was wiped out by invasions, earthquakes and floods. For more than a thousand years the Olympic Games were all but forgotten.

The elaborate Shrine of the Nymphs provided drinking-water for spectators and was put up around AD150 when the stadium was being refurbished for the last time.

Reviving the Games, Rediscovering Greece

This aerial view of Olympia shows what an enormous task it has been to excavate its remains.

The Sporting Life

Interest in competitive sport revived in Britain's top boarding schools around 1800. Their **curriculum** was based on Greek and Latin languages, literature and history. Both pupils and masters knew about the Olympics.

Like the Greeks, the British believed that games bred 'character' and gave a good training for future rulers and army officers.

In many schools sport was valued more highly than learning. The development of railways meant that travelling became easier, and this led to the growth of inter-school matches.

Gradually organizations were set up to arrange leagues and competitions, and to lay down rules for how sports were played. Unlike ancient Greek boxers, for example, modern boxers had to fight within a marked-off ring, for a limited number of rounds, with set intervals between them.

The British liking for games spread through the English-speaking world, especially in North America, Australia and Asia. American universities took the lead in developing **systematic** training and coaching.

Europe Rediscovers Olympia

The site of ancient Olympia completely disappeared under a swamp for a thousand years. It was rediscovered in 1766 by an Englishman, Richard Chandler. In 1829 a French team excavated the site for six weeks, but in that short time they only managed to dig over a small amount and prove Chandler had been right. Nothing much more came of their efforts.

In 1852 Professor Ernst Curtius of the University of Berlin gave a public lecture about Olympia. What he said was not entirely correct, but it was very interesting. Sitting in the audience was the future ruler of Germany, Kaiser Wilhelm I, who had been one of Curtius's students. Twenty years later Wilhelm made an agreement with the Greek government that a team of German scholars would undertake a full-scale excavation of Olympia, under the direction of Curtius. The work took six seasons of digging, between 1875 and 1881.

After reading about their discoveries, Pierre, Baron de Coúbertin, a young French aristocrat, was seized by a crazy idea. 'Germany,' he wrote, 'has brought to light the remains of Olympia; why should France not succeed in reviving its ancient glory?'

Did you know?

The first American Olympic team was made up of students from Harvard, Princeton, and Yale, three colleges in the 'Ivy League'. They competed in Athens, Greece, at the first modern Olympic Games which were held there in 1896.

The athletes' entrance to the stadium at Olympia. Excavation has enabled us to imagine more clearly what taking part in the Games must really have been like.

Re-inventing the Olympics

A French Crusader

Pierre de Coubertin was born on 1 January, 1863, into a wealthy French family. When he was just eight France was disastrously defeated in the Franco-Prussian war with Germany. Like many other Frenchmen, de Coubertin was haunted by the shame of that defeat. He came to believe that the disaster had been caused by a lack of fitness among French soldiers.

In German schools gymnastics was **compulsory**. The British were mad about sports. But French schools concentrated on book-learning.

Baron de Coubertin visited such famous English schools as Eton and Rugby to see their sporting life. This experience inspired him for the rest of his life as he came to believe that sport offered the best path to fitness and self-confidence. It was good for young men and good for the nations they would one day lead. Young women were not expected to become leaders.

All the members of the first International Olympic Committee were European. Baron de Coubertin is the man seated on the left.

A Greek, Spyridon Louis, winning the marathon at the Athens Olympics in 1896. The marathon was not an ancient Olympic event.

The First Modern Games

In 1889 and 1893 de Coubertin toured the USA and was impressed by the growing enthusiasm for inter-college sports. In 1894 he organized an international conference on sport in Paris and in the same year visited Olympia for the first time. The Greeks had held Olympic-style games four times between 1859 and 1889 but these had been purely local contests, almost unnoticed outside Greece.

Baron de Coubertin recruited sports enthusiasts from half a dozen different nations and won the active support of Crown Prince Constantine of Greece. He organized the first modern Olympics, which were held in Athens in 1896. The Americans fielded by far the best-prepared team of just fourteen athletes and, to the disappointment of the Greek crowd, won nine of the athletics events. Baron de Coubertin's triumph in reviving the Olympics was almost completely ignored by the French sporting newspapers.

The Struggle to Succeed

Baron de Coubertin managed to have a second Games staged in Paris in 1900, but it turned out to be a shambles, spread over five months as part of a world exhibition. At the 1904 Games, held in St Louis, almost all the competitors were American or Canadian because most other nations simply couldn't afford to travel so far. The 1908 London Games were very well organized, but the bossy British judges upset many other teams. Stockholm in 1912 finally got it right, running the Games efficiently and providing a warm welcome.

Did you know?

The Paris Games of 1900 were so badly organized that many of the contestants didn't even know that they were taking part in the Olympics!

Ancient and Modern

Baron de Coubertin's Dream

Baron de Coubertin spent so much of his own fortune promoting the Olympic movement that he died **bankrupt**. He was one of the few famous Frenchmen of his day never to have been honoured by his own country. He was, however, given a unique honour which would have meant more to him than any other could – his heart lies beneath a memorial at Olympia, de Coubertin's 'dream city'.

Although the scheduled games of 1916, 1940 and 1944 had to be cancelled because of war – unlike the ancient Games, for which truces were called – the Olympics were immediately revived after each conflict. They have survived many political and **financial** problems to become, quite simply, the sporting event which involves more of humankind than any other in the history of the entire world.

The inscription on this monument at Olympia reads 'Here lies the heart of Pierre de Coubertin'.

These stamps from Laos show how the Olympic ideal has crossed continents as well as centuries.

Continuity ...

Traces of the ancient Greek Olympics survive clearly in the modern games. Although they no longer sacrifice oxen, athletes still swear an oath to compete fairly and obey the rules and judges. Processions at the start and finish of the Games are also an important part of the proceedings. Although there are so many more events than the Greeks could ever have dreamed of, the track and field athletic contests keep their importance as the most classic events. Even if the chariot races and running in full armour have been dropped, the javelin and discus are still there and the boxing and wrestling are as popular as ever.

Did you know?

The Olympic motto – *Citius, Altius, Fortius* – is in Latin, not Greek, but the Greeks would certainly have agreed with its meaning: 'Faster, Higher, Stronger'.

... And Change

The greatest change is that women now compete in the Olympic Games. There are also symbolic changes. Olive wreaths have been replaced by medals. Hymns praising individual winners have been replaced by the anthems of the winners' countries. Releasing flights of doves at the opening ceremony, as a symbol of peace, is a reminder of the three-month truce which made it safe for people to travel to ancient Olympia.

Glossary

amateur someone who takes part in a sport just for pleasure, and is not paid for it

ambassador an official sent abroad to represent his or her country

archaeologist an expert in the science of reconstructing past ways of life from physical remains such as the ruins of buildings, tools, weapons, housewares, bones etc.

aristocrat person who belongs to a noble or important family and is usually very rich

bankrupt not having enough money to pay your debts

cauldron large pot, usually used for boiling or cooking

compulsory something which has to be done

corruption bad behaviour or dishonesty, such as cheating, bribes or threats

curriculum the list of subjects which have to be learnt by students

discus heavy circular plate of metal or stone thrown as a test of strength

drachma silver coin which was the basic unit of money or currency in ancient Greece

excavation systematic digging of a site to reveal buried objects

financial connected with money

heat an early stage in an event, from which the winners go on to the next stage

herald official appointed to make public announcements and organize ceremonies

hippodrome track for horse-racing

hygiene rules for keeping clean and healthy

lot a method of making a decision using chance, such as throwing dice or picking a card

momentum the energy or force of something or someone who is moving

oath a very solemn promise; breaking an oath brought disgrace and punishment

Olympiad four year period between Olympic Games, the basic Greek method of measuring the passing of time; sometimes used to describe the games themselves

Oracle person (usually a priestess) who represents a god and will answer questions asked of the god

pankration brutal all-in combat sport, combining boxing and wrestling

pedlar wandering salesperson

pension a regular payment made to someone when they stop working

pentathlon athletics competition involving five events – running, jumping, discus, javelin and wrestling; if a clear winner emerged early on it was sometimes unnecessary to include the wrestling; modern pentathlon has two running races and no wrestling

professional someone who makes their living from playing their chosen sport

sacrifice an offering to honour the gods, often involving the killing and burning of an animal; sacrifices could be made to ask a favour or to give thanks for one

sanitation arrangements for people to go to the toilet and keep clean

Seven Wonders of the World seven big and important buildings, statues or places that people thought were wonderful, at the time, such as the pyramids in Egypt

scholarship payment or grant made to help a student to follow a course of training

stadion measure of length used by the ancient Greeks, about 185 metres

systematic regular and organized

thong strip of leather tied into a loop and held over a finger, used by the Greeks to help them throw the javelin

tragedian actor who specializes in tragedies, plays about disastrous events

truce a short break in a war, agreed by both sides, when they stop fighting

Index

Numbers in plain type (23) refer to the text; numbers in italic (25) refer to a caption.